MAKING OF A FUTURE SAILOR AND THE ADVENTURES OF SHIP FIVE

JOSEPH OMOLLO

authorHOUSE®

AuthorHouse™
1663 Liberty Drive
Bloomington, IN 47403
www.authorhouse.com
Phone: 1 (800) 839-8640

Published by AuthorHouse 03/14/2019

ISBN: 978-1-7283-0366-6 (sc)
ISBN: 978-1-7283-0365-9 (e)

ACKNOWLEDGMENTS

Having an idea and turning it into a book is as hard as it sounds. The experience is both internally challenging and rewarding. I especially want to thank the individuals that helped make this happen. Complete thanks to AuthorHouse publishing team.

Special thanks to the United States Navy for the opportunity to enlist which gave me the motivation to put pen on paper.

To all the members of Sep team Ship 5, Momo, Mwaririe, Yun, Ajayi and all other friends that I made while in separation, thanks for all the encouragements, without you life would have been unbearable.

DEDICATION

This book is dedicated to my Mother, who taught me to never give up even when life throws bricks at you. It is also dedicated to my wife, Rachael who takes care of our son all the time I am away. To my son Gerald, who gives me motivation to wake up every morning feeling stronger.

PREFACE

The military is not meant for everyone as they say. Approximately 30 percent of recruits who enlist in the military today will not complete their full term of service. While many discharges will be for reasons beyond the recruit's control, such as medical problems that develop before/after joining the military, a significant number of the involuntary discharges imposed on first-term recruits might be because they simply stopped trying

The military can throw you out for several reasons, but you can't simply quit because you don't like it. If the military decides to throw you out (discharge you), the consequences of the discharge (depending on the type of discharge you're granted) can follow you the rest of your life.

It is advisable to have someone accompany you during your first visit to the recruiters' office. This can either be a relative, like your uncle, older brother/sisters or even your parents. This must be someone that you can confide in given that the recruiter will prompt you to respond to very personal questions, including whether you have indulged in drug abuse in the recent past, or any other personal questions that might assist in determining your qualifications

Remember that failure to get all the answers to the questions upfront might lead to consequences that might follow you the rest of your life. All recruiters are mandated to ship as many applicants as possible to the boot camp, and therefore they, in most cases will fail to disclose to the applicants some basic information that might prevent them from meeting their target of shippers for a given quarter. I would suggest you carry out your own research by exploring different public websites that talk about minimum boot camp requirements and qualifications, talk to veterans, or someone you know who's been to the boot camp before. This would assist you erase any other doubts that your recruiter might have intentionally failed to disclose to you.

MAKING OF A
FUTURE SAILOR

Future sailors hails from all corners of the world, from Africa, from the Caribbean Irelands to Europe, and all over the Great United States of America, all having a single mission of Protecting the constitution of the United states of America as well as protecting democracies all around the world.

The journey of a future sailor commences as soon as they take the initiative to visit the United States Navy recruitment offices. The offices are located within the cities of each state. At this stage the applicant gets the opportunity to talk to the recruiter, learn all the pros but never the consequences of becoming a sailor or seaman.

The recruiters will definitely tell you all the benefits you as well as your dependants stand to gain when you commit to this lifetime decision. The many tangible and intangible benefits which might include; guaranteed paycheck and cash bonuses, education benefits, advanced and specialty training, 30 days annual paid vacation, citizenship on graduating boot camp for permanent residents, traveling around the world, health and dental care, special home loans and discounts amongst others.

The applicant is then convinced that this is indeed what he wants to do, of course looking at all the benefits it would be so hard for any right thinking individual to turn down the offer. The applicant is then taken to the next stage of submitting the relevant paper work. Most applicants might take the entry level test at the recruitment office, then the final ASVAB online or at the MEPS. The questions test basically all levels of knowledge, including language, Mathematics, physics, mechanical as well as information technology. The ASVAB score is basically used to assist you choose your career in the military. Non-Prior Service applicants with ASVAB scores less than 50 must have a Tier I education status i.e... Traditional high school diploma graduate, 15 semester hours of accredited college credit or other approved avenues.

THE MEPS

The United States Military Entrance Processing Command (USMEPCOM) is responsible for ensuring applicants joining the active or reserve components of the Army, Navy, Air Force, Marines, and Coast Guard meet the standards outlined by the Department of Defense (DoD). After the selection process, the recrutiters transport their applicants to the MEPS for processing.

Before actually going to the MEPS for physical test, a recruiter will provide you with a medical prescreening form. For a majority of the "yes" answers you provide on the form, you will also need to provide the doctor and/or hospital treatment records and associated lab results.

The completed medical prescreening form and attached medical records must be forwarded to the MEPS Chief Medical Officer for review in order to gain permission to process. Once that permission is granted, then your recruiter can schedule you for your physical. If you are denied processing due to your medical history, then it may still be possible to process if the service you are applying to decides they may wish to consider a medical waiver. If denied processing by a service, you can try another. Waivers are strictly service specific. Whether these waivers are accepted at the RTC during the actual final screening of the recruits within the divisions is a story for another day. An applicant may only qualify to join any military branch by excelling with the passing score in ASVAB, as well as passing the physical and medical requirements at the MEPS.

Most applicants who's country of citizenship is not the United States might wait for a period of time (could be months or a year or more depending on the length of background investigation), before the actual shipping to the boot camp. This is to allow the investigators to successfully complete the requisite background checks and security clearances. Occasionally the recruiter will be contacting the applicants to update them of any changes in the shipping dates. This might happen once, twice or many times at the discretion of the recruiter and the MEPS.

Navy boot camp will be physically demanding, and it's important to be physically fit before you get to boot camp. You will not be able to begin your training at boot camp until you can pass the Initial Navy Fitness Assessment (IFA). To help one prepare for the boot camp, the recruiters will encourage the applicants to run the qualifying time was for their age and gender, do push-ups and sit ups. Even if you aren't good at them do them anyway. You really need to build up these muscles. If you are great at them keep doing them so you can do more. Swim, the prospective applicant needs to Learn or perfect the deadmans float for 5 min. learn how to swim in chaos. Go when the pool is the most full and practice around the most people.

THE BOOT CAMP

The United States Navy boot camp is located at Naval Station Great Lakes, North Chicago, Illinois. This is the boot camp for the enlisted. The United States Naval Academy is a four-year school for the training of officers which is located in Annapolis, Maryland.

It's normally advisable for shippers to Bring themselves, a set of clothing they don't care about (that would be what you wear, and this includes the rattiest pair of shoes you own), a change of underwear, a tooth brush, a disposable razor (if needed), and NOTHING ELSE while headed to the boot camp. Trust me on this one; you don't want to stand in the line to mail your stuff home. Bring nothing you aren't willing to toss out.

The boot camp mentality is transferred to the recruits as soon as they arrive at the Chicago Airport and meet face to face with the INSTRUCTORS who are mostly petty officers. At this point in time they are advised on how to sit and stand, how to address their trainers as well as when to walk. They are no longer at liberty to behave they way they feel, and can only talk when they are requested to respond to the questions asked.

The long awaited journey from Chicago O'Hare international airport to the Boot camp is normally embraced wit anxiety, uncertainty, fear as well as curiosity by most recruits. Most come hardly keep their eyes from gazing at the windows, wondering when the bus will stop so they can confirm all the dreaded stories they've read online or heard from their peers regarding the boot camp.

Hurry up! Get of the bus; you're too slow, line up! Stand at attention with both feet touching at the heels! That would the first encounter you get on arrival, probably from the "petty officer" welcoming you to the boot camp. You will only respond by either saying yes petty Officer, or "Yes Chief" depending on the ranks, and you only have a few seconds to figure this out.

Most recruits arrive at the boot camp through the evening to very late at night. Little do they know that they won't be having some sleep the entire night and throughout the next day. From the time of arrival and to the next day consists of various activities including issuance of necessities like PT gear, towels, bathroom and hygiene stuffs, checking of weights and height, urine tests, and issuance of the debit cards to be used for simple purchases of hygiene items from the Nex whenever you run short of them.

The night will fly by real first, followed by a gloomy day during the winter. The moment you receive the PT gear, the recruits are instructed at this juncture to change off all the civilians clothes they came, pack any other items they carried along inside a box, address it using their home address and ship them back home. The recruit is also given two minutes to make the final phone calls informing the relatives of their arrival at the boot camp, and the phone is also shipped back home along with the rest of his/her luggage. Recruits are instructed there are four pieces of information they are to relay during the phone call: they arrived safely; they will be able to make another phone call in approximately three weeks; they will be sending out a box with personal belongings; and a letter will arrive shortly containing their address and graduation information. By the next morning all the male recruits will be shaved all their hair from the head. The females have a choice of either shaving or maintaining it as stipulated by the Navy Regulations.

The worst part of Boot camp is P hold. If you arrive during a weird day or if there isn't time to get you into processing, you are put into a P hold Division. You will sit in a compartment in the Pearl Harbor (one of the "ship" barracks at boot for people in their first week) and do absolutely nothing. You might clean, you might get yelled at, but mostly you are sitting around looking at the older divisions that are closer to graduation. After you're able to go to Medical, P week begins. You've been wearing your Navy sweats and PT gear all week, so you're known as a baby div. P week involves just medical in-processing and various other activities designed to weed out anybody who isn't medically fit to make it through. Assuming you have no issues, you'll eventually get into your commissioned division. You'll then march off to your "home" for the next few weeks - one of the various ships around RTC.

From Day 1–1 on, it is basically all training (still with moderate amounts of coaching and "standing by to stand by"). The first two weeks will give you basic military knowledge. You will start to build up your knowledge to Marlinspike and weapons, weapons conditions, threat conditions, and antiterrorism. You'll move on to other subjects - firefighting, gas chamber, damage control, etc.

After you've been through enough of boot, you (and your division) will start to get the hang of things. Don't do stupid stuff - you won't get punished. Work as a team, things will be easier. Don't be an individual. Help your shipmates. Do everything you can to succeed as a unit.

Anyone who goes through boot will have their own struggles - whether it be dealing with being away from home, swimming, PT, or even learning how to fold clothes properly. You and everyone around you will be challenged in many ways. But just know that if you are really motivated, you will find the inner strength to finish. Here's a truth you will hear throughout - the fastest way out of boot camp is to graduate.

Graduation is only guaranteed on successful completion of five and a half weeks of intense training as well as scoring well on two academic tests. A recruit must also pass personnel inspection in which their appearances, knowledge are tested, compartment and gear judged as "ship-shape" during the bunk and locker inspections. The recruit must further demonstrate their ability to work as a team during fire fighting and basic seamanship. At the end of week six of training, the recruits' skills are subjected to test.

Battlestation is meant to certify the recruits' fitness, knowledge of Naval history, commitment to the team as well as their ability to apply everything they have learned while in boot camp.

On successful completion of the Battlestation the recruits are given the Navy ball cap, earning the honor to be called the "United States Sailor", and this marks the end of the training phase.

Most people who quit are stuck at boot for months doing paperwork and getting processed out of the military. That is why it is imperative to stay motivated and know YOU CAN GET THROUGH IT.

Not everyone is meant for the military and that's completely okay. If you're separated, the usual process goes like this:

- You're notified of your separation, usually by a doctor who has diagnosed you with a disqualifying medical condition, a psychologist who has diagnosed you with a disqualifying mental condition, or it came back that you failed your drug test or they found something in your past medical records that disqualifies you.
- You go back to your ship, pack up your stuff, and depending on the reason for your separation, are consoled by your Recruit Division Commanders (RDCs), such as if they diagnosed you with a condition you had no prior knowledge about. However, if you do something like fail your drug test, at least one will scold you a bit.
- You're taken to Ship 5, given sometime to call home to inform them you've been separated. This call lasts 5 minutes. Then you go unpack your stuff, and settle in. Usually within a week of being in Ship 5, you'll get an appointment to go to legal. There, you'll see your separation code, also known as you're RE Code. This will tell you if you're eligible to reenlist, if you'll need a waiver to reenlist or not, and if you can fight your case.

ADVENTURES OF SHIP 5

Recruits are normally housed in buildings referred to as Ships, synonymous with the life of sailor who spends his/her working life within the ships in the sea or ocean.

Ship 5 is also known as Div Sep, team Sep or Sep team. Sep stands for separation, meaning that at this juncture the recruit is getting separated from the United States Navy.

Ship 5 is where the Navy's rejects go. The poor souls who end up in SHIP 5, the Navy doesn't want them for some reason or another. The recruits and Sailors that get sent here are in **separation for a variety of medical reasons** including **mental health**.

Ship 5 has various sections including Bravo, Alpha, the female separation section amongst many other sections. Recruits residing in Ship 5 are mostly referred to as Seps. There are about 400 recruits in SEPS Ship at a time, between the males and the females.

For some reasons it's the only ship at the RTC without the dining launch. Seps have to walk outside in the cold during the freezing winter to get their meals at either Ship 4 or 6.

The first obvious way that a recruit will become a Sep is through medical separation during the P-days. This happens when a recruit fails the eye test, ear test, as well as many other medical condition including asthma. Medical separation can still take place at any time during the training as long as the medicals discover something from a recruits past life that might jeopardize his health condition while he/she is serving, or when a recruit develops a condition during the training that the Navy thinks doesn't meet the requisite health standard.

The second ticket to ship 5 is mental or psychological separation. This happens when a recruit is diagnosed with unspecified anxiety disorder which might emanate from so many unknown conditions. For instance, I have had of recruit who was separated and diagnosed with unspecified anxiety disorder due to a fit of random shaking at Red Rover. He later learned it was a temporary incident triggered by high levels of salt during the meals; as he was on low-sodium diet to keep water weight off before shipping out. Yet another recruit also got separated because they were allergic to peanut butter. Many recruits always get separated for depression, anxiety, PTSD, ADHD, CRYING, BEING

ANGRY. The truth is these kids are sleep deprived, just got yelled at and are being interviewed in a high pressure environment. They think they can relax and vent in the therapist office because they are told they can, but they really can't. Most recruits come to RTC at a tender age of 17-20 years. At this stage of their lives they are just fresh from high school, and are still trying to discover themselves. Majority of them are usually still living under their parents roofs, some have never been home for such a long time.

Other tickets to ship 5 might include legal separations, like failing the minimum physical requirements to qualify for training, failing urinalysis tests and medical board separation.

Ship 5 also houses THU sailors. THU Sailors are Sailors who have graduated from Recruit Training Command and are awaiting follow-on orders to their A school. The reasons for placing a graduated Sailor on hold can vary from clearance issues to the need for special physicals. Sometimes it is as simple as waiting for a class to fill up.

These Sailors, however, are not just waiting around. THU Sailors follow a daily schedule. Many THU Sailors maintain work assignments while awaiting their follow-on orders, to include: manning the Ship, acting as escorts for recruits transiting to medical or legal appointments, or performing office duties at locations throughout the base.

THU Sailors are housed in separate compartments from separating recruits, with males on the lower deck and females on the upper deck.

THU Sailors also enjoy more liberty time, and are permitted to leave the base for recreation or visiting with family members. They may call home in their free time.

LIFE AT SHIP 5 BRAVO

Seps at Ship 5 Bravo go through the same routine as other Seps in the divisions. This includes waking up early as required and making their racks using the RTC format. Most hygiene is normally conducted after the last meal of the day. The time of waking up may or vary depending on whether a Sep has an early appointment the next day.

Life can be very challenging for Seps at Bravo. For some reasons, There is normally scarcity of tissue/ toilet papers which makes some Seps to grab and keep some napkins during their meal times to be used later as toilet papers. Illinois is also extremely cold during the winter and temperatures can go as low as negative 30 degrees, and the fact that Sep save to walk outside all the times for meals make s almost all of them susceptible to the flue which quickly spreads like wildfire amongst them.

Bravo has rotational self appointed leaders from the Seps themselves referred to as MAs. In most cases these MAs exercises their powers to bully their fellow Seps. For instance failure to follow simple instructions from the MAs might lead to various consequences like getting reported to the Unit Coordinators (UCs), getting punishments which might include sweeping the decks for several hours or sitting on the cold deck for up to 3hours at the discretion of the UC.

There's also scarcity of chairs in Bravo, and no one is allowed to rest on their racks during the day. This means that the Seps in Bravo spend most of their time sitting on the cold deck or standing during the day.

Get off your racks! Wake-up! That would be the usual morning wake-up call for another day from the UC on duty in Bravo. The time is probably 4:30 am, 5:00 am or 5:30 am as the UC wishes. The routine is as usual; put on the uniform of the day which would be a watch cap, scarf, neck getter, **Navy** Working Uniform (NWU), Boots etcetera. This will be followed by cleaning on the deck and lining up for breakfast.

It is often frustratingly boring in Ship 5 Bravo, but we did get to watch movies frequently, go to the Navy Exchange (NEX) every other day to make phone calls and but hygiene stuffs, conducting banking transactions at Navy Credit Union and having plenty of books and magazines to read. Everything is considerably more relaxed than actual training. However, many of us are quietly bitter because our dreams were crushed. There has been mentions of attempted suicide cases by some Seps while in Bravo. You are still expected to wear your uniform, keep your bed made with the exception of the 90 degree corners, and keep an organized rack. Going to the NEX, watching TV or getting to the launch can however be secured on multiple occasions. All it takes is one person fucking up/ making a mess. At which point we basically all have to sit quietly for extended periods of time. That is referred to as being secured and is absolutely awful. It's pretty easy to make friends in Bravo.

Meal times, also referred to as Chow times, are usually relaxed, with the Recruit Chief Petty Officer (RCOP) yelling "Good morning division, today will be dining at table 1, 2, and 3, we line in both child lines, starting on the fourth side of table One, please don't forget the hand sanitizer..". Te menu is almost the same as the previous day, where you get sample you delicacies, not forgetting the drinks.

Muster has to be read every time you get back to the compartment. This is usually for accountability to ensure that no one is missing from the division. On a good day, a few names will be read from the departure list to leave Bravo for Alpha, creating more space in the racks to be filled by in-coming Seps to Bravo. On each we are left with memories of the those who were lucky to leave Bravo, always hoping that your name will be in the departure list for the next day, if at all their would be a list.

LIFE AT SHIP 5 ALPHA
AND DEPARTING
FROM BOOT CAMP

After going for in-dock and legal and refuting to fight for your case, the next phase is usually just a game of waiting for the departure date to leave the boot camp. Most Seps waiting for their departure date are normally transferred from Bravo to Alpha.

For some reasons, Alpha is more organized than Bravo, with even less tension and animosity between the Seps. The UCs in Alpha are more friendly to Seps than in Alpha. The daily routines are almost same as Bravo, but with more opportunities to sit on chairs, watch lots of movies and participate in some leisure activities compared to Bravo.

Departure date is usually given at least a week before one leaves the boot camp. This is due to the many number of Seps, and the NAVY has to make all these arrangements for the flight booking to all these destinations.

Most Seps are however never prepared to go back to the civilian life, given that they came to the boot camp with a high hope for a perfect future and suddenly, the dreams were cut short in Ship five.

I went to the boot camp at the age of 37 (actually I was amongst the oldest recruits in boot camp). It took me two years to ship to the boot camp, since a lot of background check was being conducted during the two-year wait given that am a permanent resident. I was working two jobs before making a decision to join the NAVY. One of my major decisions was to serve this beloved country where my son is a proud citizen. Like my fellow immigrants, I thought it was also an opportunity to expedite my citizenship process. Other benefits like medical insurance, MGI educational assistance programmes, as well other monetary incentives further influenced my decision to join the Navy.

I went through the process and was given a waiver by MEPS for my eyes while headed to the boot camp. My recruiters did not inform me at any given time that separations happen in the Navy. My only worry was therefore passing the physical test at boot camp, and I therefore did a lot of morning and evening runs and was able to lose 8 pounds within one week of shipping.

I got separated at P3 week one of the boot camp during the eye test. It came as a shock to me, knowing how much I had sacrificed, and how long I had waited for this. I was therefore determined to fight for my case when I got to Ship 5, knowing that there was a copy of the waiver in the medical records. My opinion however changed as soon as I was in Bravo and was given orientation by the "wise Seps" of Bravo. They narrated to me that we're still legally veterans (most of us that were separated don't like assigning that title to ourselves though), explained that the purpose of Ship 5 is to adjust you back to civilian life, that we can expect to be there for at least a 10-21 days) and that it's mostly a lot of hurry up and wait, and that there's everyone's time which will be on a case by case basis. If you choose to fight your case to go back to training, you can expect to be there AT LEAST a month and usually more. I pondered over the issue for the first two nights and something miraculous happened that propelled me to the decision of not fighting my case.

I met Momo on my second day in Bravo. Momo was 35 years old and also a permanent resident like me. Further discussion with Momo filled me with the hopes that I was actually not alone in the struggle. Like me, he had a master's degree and joined the Navy for same reasons that made me enlist. While in Bravo he was acting as the Rack PO and was liked by most Seps because he was friendly and mature. He got separated during week six of he's training after being diagnosed with Asthma. Momo Believed that he's never had the symptoms before and therefore the Navy had an error with his diagnosis. According to him, it was the cold in Illinois that was making him show the signs of Asthma, and therefore he had the conviction that he would win his case. When I first met him, he had stayed in Bravo for 47 days, almost the same amount of time he had spend while on training with the division, and still waiting for the decision of the legal panel. It therefore came as a shock the following week when Momos' name alongside others who were fighting for their case was read in the next departure list. He confided in me that he can only re-enlist as an officer, and had learned from his mistake.

There was also Mwaririe from Virginia who joined the Navy to expedite his citizenship process, as well as other benefits that come along with serving. He got separated during the P-week after the eye diagnosis. He never knew of his eye condition until the test in boot camp revealed. He was also disappointed because the recruiters never disclosed to him that he might get separated of anything apart from completing the required 1.5 mile run and the pushups. He had a wife and two kids, and was not fighting his case, but would re-enlist if given a chance with any other military branch.

Yun was from Dallas, Texas, 35 years of age and was also married with two kids. He had enlisted for various reasons and was separated after one month of training due to anxiety and depression. Yun acted as a laundry team member in Alpha, and I must confess that he was the most prayerful person I had met, keeping all his daily prayer requests in a notebook that he guarded closely. I shared a rack while in Alpha with Yun. He was also not fighting his case and was happy to have received his departure date.

Ajayi was also over 30 years from New Jersey. He had been separated after experiencing chest pain in the third week of training. He felt like he had discovered so many things his recruiters never disclosed to him during enlistment, and was therefore not fighting his case. He had a master's degree, and given a second chance he would only re-enlist as an officer.

Talking to all these friendly Seps I met in Ship 5, and listening to their stories greatly influenced my decision when I went for legal. I knew I was not going to fight my case since I envisioned what the outcome would be. The single person that I witnessed while in Ship 5 getting recalled back to training was Song. He had been in separation for close to two months and was in charge of the watch list during my last week in Alpha. After completely his treatment he was cleared to get back to training, and I believe he will make a brave sailor once he graduates boot camp given the way he shined his boots!

I stayed in Seps for four weeks, but I was lucky to have spend only a week in Bravo, while the remainder of my time in Alpha. I felt anxious each and every single day that my name was missing in the departure list. I kept pestering the UCs with questions on whether there would be another list the following day, and if it was a mistake that my name was skipped. I had a feeling that Legal had misplaced my records. At some point I even told my fellow Seps that I was planning an escape route, even though I knew the consequences of making a dumb decision like that. One of the UCs had even hinted to us that the Navy would not prevent you from escaping. But he further mentioned that, "we will look for you in your mothers' house, and we will find you, and you will regret the decision for the remainder of your life"!

I therefore felt a sigh of relief of learning my departure date, even though I knew the week that followed was going to be the longest in my entire life. I was ready to rejoin the civilian world, and above everything, I was missing my wife and son more than anything else in the world. Getting separated makes one feel like your entire world has crushed, and the dreams shuttered. You therefore need a strong reason to keep believing that its not the end of the road after all. Especially if you put in a lot of sacrifices, preparation and waited for a long time before shipping out.

I spend the remaining days reading more novels and watching lots of movies. I read about dictatorship in N. Korea and how a journalist sought asylum in S. Korea. I read about World War II and the bombings of Ships in Nagasaki. I also read about Pakistan and Afghanistan and the manufacture of Nuclear weapons. But above all I continued writing this book so that I can also narrate a story to book readers. I also volunteered as a Trash P.O as well as a road guard for the six days of my final week.

Once you get your departure date, you normally get te opportunity to liquidate your laundry as well as the eagle cards, which can get you a few bucks to your pocket. The day before my departure was the day of my departure brief. I remember waking up in disbelief that I only had three meals left and I will on my way out. It was usual for Seps with the departure date to count how many meals were remaining before they could leave the boot camp. We were quite a big number I must say who were scheduled for a brief on this particular day. The brief takes you through various stages as I came to witness. To begin with, you are given the itinerary for your flight which just shows the flight date, time as well as the name of the airline. The destination of the flight is usually to the closest airport near your home, or the airport you dept in while shipping to the boot camp.

The next phase of the departure brief involves meeting the chiefs one by one and explaining your reason for separation and what type of preparations you were making to enable you come back to the boot camp, if at all one was planning to give it another shot!

The final phase of departure brief is where you're handed the summary packet of your separation from the Navy. This packet contains all legal documents detailing the cause of separation, as well as the code that determines if one eligible for re-enlistment. The packet also contains some financial settlement, which is just the salary for the last month in separation with huge deductions for the uniforms you were issued on your arrival to the boot camp.

It is also on this day that the Navy will secure almost 80% of the uniforms you were issued, apart from the Physical training gear that you will wear while departing the boot camp.

On the day of departure, you wake up at 3:00 AM. The roving security watch is usually tasked with waking up everyone that's departing on this day. After a quick hygiene, muster is read to confirm that everyone is awake, you then line up by the quarter deck or sit by the pee-way by 4:45 AM. The next process is then signing out with Chief of the deck in Ship 5, where you also state for the final time your reason for separation.

You finally get another opportunity to board the bus that brought you to the boot camp one more time. Only that this time there's no Petty Officer to escort you out, and no one bothers on how you sit inside the bus, whether male and/or female. There's a sigh of relief as the bus departs the gate. Every one can feel some freedom in the air. Freedom from coughing, freedom from sitting down for couple of hours, freedom from MAs, freedom from the tiny racks and above all the freedom from freezing Illinois cold.

I was privileged to get back my part-time job. I spent three more weeks treating the flue and the backaches that I had developed while in Ship 5. As I was finishing writing this book I was still trying to reapply to my full-time job, if only they still had an opening to take me back, given how hardworking I was before I left, knowing that I also left in good books.

CONCLUSION

Every single week there are new shippers to the boot camp and every single day there are new admissions of Seps to ship 5. Majority of these Seps are mostly victims of circumstances that they're caused to remember for their entire life. Most of these cases could however be avoided in the earliest, if only some people were more efficient at their jobs, or if care could be taken while performing the final tests before sipping to boot camp.

One of the Seps in Ship 5 Bravo confided to me that he quit the difficult street life with the high hopes of a second chance in life while serving in the Navy. But given that he was separated, he was unsure of what was in store for him in the civilian world.

Good programmes need to be put in place to assist the Seps transition back to the civilian life.

I would recommend some short introduction to computer packages like learning to use Ms-Word, PowerPoint presentation, or Ms-Excel basics for those who are computer illiterate. Career advice, training on the use of forklift as well as pallet jacks are some of the simple tools that can easily be taught to these Seps as a means of preparing them for the job in the civilian world.

Fair treatment and lack of discrimination on the Seps by all parties at RTC must also be encouraged. For instances, I remember at the Navy Credit Union where recruits in divisions are given first priority over Seps, with a mere excuse that they are needed back to the division by their RDCs! I interpreted the statement to mean, no one needs the Seps anyway, only when you are required for a working party.

To all the recruits who successfully graduate boot camp, to all the sailors out there, thank you for your service to make this world a better place. Everyday we get to live our lives in freedom because of you all.

For the Seps whose dreams were cut short in Ship 5, just know that the sky is never the limit, and keep aiming beyond the Sky. There's always a reason for all misfortunes. Use the challenge as a stepping stone to more opportunities. As Alexander Graham Bell once stated that "When one door closes, another opens; but we often look so long and so regretfully upon the closed door that we do not see the one which has opened for us." Our relationships all serve some sort of purpose...even if it's just to get us to the next relationship...or the next step on our life's journey.

Printed in the United States
By Bookmasters